W9-BTO-421

THE SWEDES IN AMERICA

The IN AMERICA *Series*

The CZECHS *and* SLOVAKS *in America*
The DUTCH *in America*
The EAST INDIANS *and* PAKISTANIS *in America*
The ENGLISH *in America*
The FRENCH *in America*
The GERMANS *in America*
The GREEKS *in America*
The HUNGARIANS *in America*
The IRISH *in America*
The ITALIANS *in America*
The JAPANESE *in America*
The JEWS *in America*
The NEGRO *in America*
The NORWEGIANS *in America*
The POLES *in America*
The SCOTS *and* SCOTCH-IRISH *in America*
The SWEDES *in America*
The FREEDOM OF THE PRESS *in America*
The FREEDOM OF RELIGION *in America*
The FREEDOM OF SPEECH *in America*

We specialize in publishing quality books for
young people. For a complete list please write:

LERNER PUBLICATIONS COMPANY
241 First Avenue North, Minneapolis, Minnesota 55401

The IN AMERICA *Series*

THE SWEDES IN AMERICA

PERCIE V. HILLBRAND

Elementary School Supervisor for
Minnesota State Department of
Education (Retired)

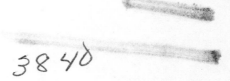

3840

Published by
Lerner Publications Company
Minneapolis, Minnesota

ACKNOWLEDGEMENTS

The illustrations are reproduced through the courtesy of: p. 6, Swedish Information Service; p. 9, The Smithsonian Institution, Division of Numismatics; pp. 11, 28, 43 (left), Post Office Department, Division of Philately; pp. 13, 15, 18, Delaware State Archives; pp. 16, 17, 46 (left), 59 (right), 62, The American-Swedish News Exchange; pp. 21, 23 (left), 35, 41 (left), 56, Minnesota Historical Society; pp. 23 (right), 43 (right), 44 (top), Library of Congress; pp. 24 (left and right), 26, 57 (bottom left), Independent Picture Service; p. 27, Galvaland Press; p. 31, U. S. Immigration and Naturalization Service; p. 33, Stockholm National Museum; p. 39 (top left and right, bottom left and right), Walgreen Drug Stores; p. 40, Matson Lines; p. 41 (right), Greyhound Corporation; pp. 44 (bottom left and right), 45 (top), Stromberg-Carlson Corporation; p. 45 (bottom left), The Bendix Corporation; p. 45 (bottom right), General Electric Company; p. 46 (right), U. S. Atomic Energy Commission; p. 48, The Boeing Company; p. 49, The Bettman Archive; p. 51 (left), Gustavus Adolphus College; p. 51 (right), Upsala College; p. 53 (left and right), The University of Iowa; p. 57 (top), United Press International; p. 57 (bottom right), U. S. Department of Agriculture; pp. 58 (left and right), 59 (left), Office of the Senator; p. 65, Mayo Clinic; pp. 67 (left and right), 68 (top left and right), Metropolitan Opera Archives; pp. 68 (bottom left and right), 69, (top left and right), 76, TV Times; p. 69 (bottom left), Station KSTP, Minneapolis; p. 69 (bottom right), Station WCCO, Minneapolis; p. 70 (left), The Baltimore Museum of Art; p. 70 (right), Percie V. Hillbrand; p. 73, St. Paul Area Chamber of Commerce. The quotation on p. 54 is from *Americans from Sweden* by Adolph B. Benson and Naboth Hedin, published by J. B. Lippincott Company.

Fourth Printing 1969

International Copyright Secured. Printed in U.S.A.
Standard Book Number: 8225-0201-1
Library of Congress Catalog Card Number: AC 66-10152

...CONTENTS...

PART I. European Background

1. *The Land Called Sweden* 7
2. *The Climate of Sweden* 8
3. *The People in Sweden* 8
4. *Conditions in Sweden 1611-1660* 11
5. *Founding of the Swedish Colony in America* 14

PART II. Swedish Immigration to America

1. *Conditions in Sweden in the 1800's* 19
2. *Advantages in America* 22
3. *Immigration to the North Central States* 23
4. *Immigration to Other Sections of the
    United States* 29
5. *High and Low Points in Immigration* 31

PART III. Swedish Contributions to American Life

1. *Agriculture* 34
2. *Business, Trade, Manufacturing* 37
3. *Engineering, Science and Invention* 42
4. *Education* 50
5. *Government and Politics* 54
6. *Literature and the Press* 60
7. *Medicine* 63
8. *Music and Entertainment* 66
9. *Artists and Sculptors* 70
10. *Religion and Religious Leaders* 74

CONCLUSION 79

The Swedes led by Peter Minuit arrive in Delaware Bay,
March 1638, to found a colony.

PART I.

European Background

1. *The Land called Sweden*

As we look at the map of Europe we find a peninsula in the extreme northwestern part called Scandinavia. This peninsula contains two countries — Norway which occupies the western part and Sweden in the eastern part. It is the country of Sweden, its people, and their American descendants, that we will read about in this book.

This land called Sweden extends from 55° North Latitude to about 70° North Latitude. The southernmost part is as far north as Labrador in North America and the frozen wastelands of Siberia in Asia. Fifteen percent of Sweden lies north of the Arctic Circle.

The area of Sweden is 173,403 square miles. This is about as big as the states of Illinois, Kentucky, Ohio, and Indiana put together. The surface can be divided into three sections. The northern part has mountains, narrow deep valleys, swift rivers, and many lakes. The middle and southern sections are covered with forests of Scotch pine and Norway spruce. The land is fairly level, but broken with a few rocky highlands and rolling hills. Here we find many rivers and the largest lakes in Sweden.

The middle section contains the rich deposits of iron ore for which Sweden is famous. This region is also the most scenic. The southern section and the plains of Skane contain very fertile soil which is easily tilled. It is Sweden's chief agricultural area.

2. *The Climate of Sweden*

The great length of Sweden, which is about 1000 miles from North to South, causes much difference in climate, plant life, and the way people live in the various provinces.

Temperatures vary greatly from the northernmost province of Lapland to that of Skane in the South. Summers are short and winters are long in the entire country. Snow falls everywhere in Sweden. It remains on the ground 50 days in Skane and from 170 to 190 days in Karesuand, the northernmost city.

The average yearly rainfall varies from 18 inches on the Baltic Sea Coast to 28 inches on the southernmost coast. Most of the rain falls in the late summer and early fall.

On the whole, the climate of Sweden is sunnier and drier than Norway and other countries in the same latitude. This is due to the winds from the West which bring warm air as they blow across the Gulf Stream in the Atlantic Ocean. The many lakes also help to keep the climate more temperate. The climate of Sweden promotes excellent forest growth and makes farming more productive than it is in the neighboring countries.

3. *The People in Sweden*

The present population of Sweden, according to the 1960 census, is about 7,500,000 people. This is an increase of slightly more than 5½ million since 1750. The natural increase is slow because Sweden has one of the lowest birthrates of any country in the world.

During the 19th century (the 1800's) the birthrate decreased more rapidly than the deathrate. The cause for this was the immigration of young people and their families to America. You will read elsewhere in this book how this migration almost depopulated some provinces in Sweden between 1880 and 1900.

The northern two-thirds of the country contain only one-sixth of the population and many large areas are uninhabited. This is due to the ruggedness of the land and the cold climate. More than one-half of the people live in the central lowlands from Stockholm to

Gothenberg. It is in this region that all the large cities and most of the industries are located.

Sixty-five percent of the people live in cities and 34 percent live in rural areas. The density of population is about 43 people per square mile. Spain, which has about the same area as Sweden, has a density of 154 people per square mile. We can see that Sweden is not overpopulated.

In recent years the population shift from rural areas to the cities has continued at a high rate. Fewer people are needed in agriculture today and more are needed in manufacturing and service occupations because Sweden is rapidly becoming an important industrial nation.

Practically all the people are pure Swedes. Their ancestors have lived in Sweden for thousands of years. Their physical characteristics, fair skin and hair, blue eyes, and tall stature, show that there has not been much intermarriage with other races and nationalities.

During the Middle Ages and succeeding centuries there was some immigration into Sweden. These people were for the most part German, Dutch, Jews, Russians, and some Italian traders. Traces of those can be seen in the dark hair and brown eyes of

The Delaware Tercentenary half-dollar, issued to commemorate the 300th anniversary of the landing of the Swedes in Delaware. The two sides show the colonists' ship, the *Kalmar Nyckel*, and the Old Swedes Church.

the people living along the Baltic Sea. As one travels inland these characteristics disappear.

Swedish is closely related to the Danish, Norwegian, and Icelandic languages. Originally all the Germanic tribes in northern Europe spoke a common language with a few variations. Old Norse, as that speech is called, dates back to the 3rd century, A.D. The four different Scandinavian languages began in the Viking Period, about A.D. 800. Today many of the people speak English and German.

It is important to know something about the religion of the Swedish people, for it played a part in the emigration from Sweden to the United States.

The first Christian religion in Sweden was Catholic. This was brought into the country during the time of the Romans by the Christian missionary St. Ansgar. It was not until after the Reformation in Europe in the early 1500's that the Lutheran faith was adopted and became the state religion of Sweden. For several centuries no other religious belief was allowed. If the people objected to the practices of the State Church and accepted other forms of worship they were persecuted or sent out of the country. Today that law has been changed and other religious denominations are permitted. Unless a native born Swede formally withdraws, however, he remains a member of the State Church for life.

The church is supported by the government through taxes. Although other religious denominations exist, about 90 percent of the people are members of the Lutheran Church.

The origin of the Swedish people is not known. The land called Scandinavia was inhabited as early as 12,000 B.C. These people developed a high degree of civilization. The Roman Empire had trade relations with Scandinavia. Merchants from Sweden established trade routes and trade centers in Russia and the Far East many years before the Crusades. In the 8th century Sweden figured prominently in the history of Europe.

Much has been written about the characteristics of the Swedes. Whether these apply to all is questionable. However, there are

U.S. postage stamp issued to mark the 300th anniversary of the landing of the Swedes in 1638.

certain traits which have been common among those of Swedish descent. They have the pioneer spirit, that is, a willingness to work and endure hardships to accomplish a worthwhile goal. They adapt themselves quickly to new environments. They are healthy, strong, and enjoy nature. In the United States they have been called "dumb Swedes," because their reactions have been slow. The reason for this was their desire to be sure before attempting to perform a task or solve a problem. The Swedes are naturally adventurous, daring, and courageous. They love order, justice, cleanliness, and beauty. They have a high reputation for honesty, politeness, industry, and intelligence. They surely deserve to be called progressive people.

4. *Conditions in Sweden 1611-1660*

Up to the beginning of the 17th century Sweden had been fighting wars with neighboring lands almost constantly for several hundred years. These wars had drained the country of most of its wealth. Trade was almost at a standstill. Manufacturing had been neglected. The nation was in a sad state of affairs.

It was at this time that Spanish, Dutch, and English merchants were conducting successful trade with America and had brought wealth to their countries in Europe. The rulers of Sweden looked with envy upon those trading companies. Swedish merchants had been active in trade with the Turks and the people of the Far East before the Crusades. Now their foreign trade and shipping was limited to the cities on the Baltic Sea. The reason for this was that Denmark had control of all the ports leading to the Atlantic Ocean

11

and the Swedes and Danes at this time were bitter enemies.

In 1613 Sweden paid a large sum for the harbor and fortress Elfsborg at the mouth of the Gota River on the west coast. To obtain this money, practically every inhabitant in Sweden was taxed. This was a great hardship on the people.

As soon as the King gained possession of the fortress he built Gothenburg a few miles further up the river, and invited Dutch builders and merchants to help develop the city. He also wanted the Dutch to assist in developing foreign trade for Sweden.

The first company organized was not successful due to a war which broke out between the Protestants and Catholics in the German States. Sweden entered the war on the Protestant side. King Gustavus Adolphus was the leader of the Swedish army. On November 6, 1632, he was killed in the battle of Lutzen.

The heir to the throne was the King's infant daughter, Christina. The real ruler, however, was Count Axel Oxenstierna. Shortly after Count Oxenstierna became the head of the government in Sweden, Peter Minuit, the first governor of New Amsterdam and the man who purchased Manhattan Island from the Indians, came to Stockholm. He had been dismissed from the Dutch West India Company and was looking for a chance to organize a rival trading company.

Several wealthy merchants in Sweden and Holland agreed to form a company and finance it. In addition to trade, the company agreed to establish a Swedish colony in America.

Two second-hand ships, the *Kalmar Nyckel,* a merchant ship, and the *Fogel Grip,* a naval vessel, were obtained to make the first voyage to America. On board were 23 Swedish soldiers, and a crew which was half Dutch and half Swedish. A Dutchman, named Hendrick Huygen, had charge of the goods to be traded to the Indians for beaver skins and tobacco. Peter Minuit was general manager of the sailing expedition.

The preparations took a long time so it was not until late in August of 1637 that the ships left Stockholm. It took one month to reach Gothenburg on the west coast where more goods were put on board.

On November 20th the expedition finally started across the Atlantic. By the end of March 1638, they arrived safely in what is now known as Delaware Bay. They proceeded up the Delaware River until they came to the mouth of a tributary known as Minquas. According to directions and instructions from the company, they then sailed up this river for two miles and landed on the west bank. Here Minuit and his men stepped ashore on a large flat-topped rock. Today this spot is marked by a monument of black granite and is on the waterfront of the city of Wilmington, Delaware.

The Carl Milles' sculpture of the *Kalmar Nyckel* at the Fort Christina Monument, Wilmington, Delaware.

5. *Founding of the Swedish Colony in America*

Peter Minuit lost no time in securing land from the Indians. A contract was made and signed by five Indian chiefs, who agreed to trade all the land on the west bank of the river. This is the area where the city of Philadelphia stands today. The Indians told Minuit he could take as much land to the west as he wished. To the Indians the value of land consisted in the right to pass over it and to hunt and fish on it. Land to them was like the ocean. It was limitless and there was plenty for everyone.

Formal possession of the land was made by raising the Swedish flag on a pole and firing a salute. This land was given the name *New Sweden.* A stronghold was built as a defense against wild animals and human enemies. It was given the name Fort Christina in honor of Princess Christina, who later became the Queen of Sweden.

Trading with the Indians was begun at once. This was carried on by the Dutch. When spring came the men dug up some of the ground around the fort and planted wheat and barley. The Swedes knew nothing about trading with Indians but they did know how to plant crops.

In June of 1638 Peter Minuit with a crew and 700 beaver skins set sail on the *Kalmar Nyckel* for Sweden. Minuit, however, died a short time afterwards. He was killed in the West Indies while visiting on a Dutch ship. This was a serious loss to the new Swedish settlement.

The *Kalmar Nyckel* was welcomed on its arrival in Sweden although the cargo of furs didn't pay half of the expenses of the expedition. However, the reports of the fertile farm lands, the warm, invigorating climate, and the abundance of wild game and fish were encouraging to the Swedish people.

When the *Kalmar Nyckel* was ready to return to America, it had on board farm implements, horses, cattle, foodstuffs, ammunition, farmhands, and goods for trading with the Indians. The members of the company were eager to make New Sweden an agricultural as well as a trading colony.

Peter Ridder, another Dutchman, was appointed governor to succeed Peter Minuit. He was instructed to purchase more land from the Indians. This he proceeded to do and bought land on both sides of the river as far north as the falls at Trenton and as far south as Cape May.

The trade which the company expected from New Sweden was disappointing and the Dutch stockholders wanted to withdraw. In the fall of 1641 they were paid off. The government of Sweden then bought one-sixth of the shares. The company now became an enterprise owned jointly by private stockholders and the kingdom of Sweden.

About the same time as the government invested money in the colony, more people were sent to New Sweden. Among them were a tailor, a blacksmith, and a clergyman. More horses, cattle, sheep, goats, and farm tools were also sent over. New settlements were formed and Lieut. Col. Johan Printz, a Swede, was appointed the governor. He was efficient, aggressive, and full of energy, but at times hotheaded and pompous. He was about seven feet tall and weighed almost 400 pounds. He was a military man and ruled with an iron hand.

Johan Printz was the third governor, and the first Swede, to govern New Sweden, 1645-1655.

15

As soon as Governor Printz came to New Sweden he ordered the building of several new villages. Three additional forts were built along the river to control trade. This expansion alarmed the Dutch, who claimed some of the land and had plans for trade with the Indians in that area.

The Indians in their eagerness for trade with the white men had sold the same pieces of land to the Dutch that earlier they had sold to the Swedes, and trouble soon arose between the two groups. Governor Printz appealed to Sweden for more men and ships to protect the colony but received none. Finally the Dutch under Peter Stuyvesant seized Ft. Casimir, which was the Swedes' most important stronghold. Later, having received more troops from Holland, Peter Stuyvesant captured Ft. Christina, for the Dutch soldiers far outnumbered the Swedish defenders.

Thus ended Sweden's attempt to plant a colony in America. From that time the few Swedish settlers who came to America

The John Hendrickson house in Wilmington, Delaware, built by Swedish colonists in the 18th century.

settled in the English colonies and were content to live under the rule already established there.

Although the Swedish colony was not a success the Swedes made some contributions to Colonial America. They made the first permanent settlement in the Delaware River Valley. The colony was small but well managed. No slaves were allowed in it and the settlers were on friendly terms with the Indians. They brought over the first Lutheran ministers, built the first churches, the first flour mills, the first permanent homes, and the first roads in what is now Delaware and parts of Pennsylvania. They built the first real log cabins in the colonies. They made maps of the region, set up the first organized government and introduced both the court and jury system. The instructions given to Johan Printz when he became Governor of New Sweden was the first written law of the colony. By these and other contributions, the Swedish colonists helped prepare the way for William Penn when he came in 1682 and founded the colony of Pennsylvania.

Interior of the John Hendrickson house.

The Swedish people who had settled in New Sweden remained there even though they were under Dutch rule for a period of time and later came under the rule of the English. Swedish clergymen were sent over to serve in the Lutheran churches that had been built. They were instructed by the State Church of Sweden to build better and more lasting churches for the colonists. These men kept Sweden well informed about America. They also helped the Swedish botanists, geologists, and scientists who came over to the colonies to study the flora and fauna of the new country.

As time went on the Swedish colonists intermarried with the Dutch and the English so traces of the first settlers in New Sweden are difficult to find. Even the churches ceased to be Lutheran and became affiliated with the English Episcopal churches. However we do know that two descendants of the original Swedish colonists became prominent during the American Revolution. They are mentioned in another chapter.

Old Swedes Church, built in 1698; the oldest Protestant church still in use in the U.S.

PART II.

Swedish Immigration to America

1. *Conditions in Sweden in the 1800's*

During the first half of the 19th century there was much unrest among the people in Sweden. There were many reasons for this. The majority of the people worked on farms because agriculture was the chief industry of the country. As was mentioned earlier, large areas of Sweden are not suitable for growing crops. In addition to that, much of the best land had been held for centuries by the nobility and wealthy land owners. Most of this good land was in the southern provinces where the population was the most dense. There was little chance for anyone in the middle or lower classes to buy land. That which was for sale was too expensive. As a rule the land and the estate were passed on to the oldest son when the father died. This left younger sons without any property.

The rural districts were overpopulated, so wages for farm laborers were very low. Taxes were high, not only on land but also on personal property. Industrialization and manufacturing were just beginning, so there were not enough jobs for everyone who wanted to work. All these conditions kept many people very poor.

From 1867 to 1869 there were serious crop failures in Sweden. This, together with overpopulation, caused an agricultural depression. Times were hard and many people had very little food to eat during those years.

About the same time that Sweden was having the agricultural depression many people, especially in the northern provinces, were beginning to object to the rigid rules imposed upon them by the State Church and its clergymen. The State Church was Lutheran and the government ruled the church. As soon as a child was born in Sweden, he became a member of the Lutheran Church. He had to remain a member and pay taxes to the church as long as he lived. No person was allowed to belong to any other religious denomination or worship in any other place except in a Lutheran church. No other church was allowed in Sweden.

Many of the clergymen ruled the people in their parishes like dictators. They demanded heavy taxes from the parishioners and kept most of it for their own use. Oftentimes the clergy were intemperate in their living habits. The people did not feel they were true spiritual leaders. All these disagreements caused the people to leave the church and form new religious groups. Among these dissenters were the Janssonites, Luther Readers, and the Mission Friends.

About the same time that these separatist movements began, Methodist and Baptist preachers from Great Britain came to Sweden. These missionaries were forbidden to preach and the people were forbidden to attend their meetings. However, meetings were held in secret and people flocked to hear the missionary preachers. In order to stop this movement against the State Church, many of the dissenters' leaders were put in jail and some were sent out of the country. The results of this controversy will be discussed later.

Although there had never been any slavery or serfdom in Sweden there was much class distinction. The nobility received their title by birth. This did not necessarily mean that they were wealthy, but because of their heritage they had certain privileges in the government, in the army, and in the church.

The gentry were the people who owned large estates and they too had certain privileges. The government officials and the educated clergy who lived in every community considered themselves very much above the peasant class. The peasants and small farmers felt themselves much above the landless renters and farm laborers. This class system did not allow the freedoms, social and economic, that we enjoy in the United States.

In addition to social inequality there was much political inequality. The right to vote and to hold public office was based on the amount of land a person owned. This deprived many of the peasants and the lower classes of voting rights. A laborer had no right to vote whatsoever. There was no freedom of speech, press, or assembly. All able-bodied young men had to take military training when they became 20 years of age. They were required to spend three months each year for three years in army camps. This training was rigid and harsh. The discipline was severe. The people in the rural areas objected to their loss of freedom.

All of the conditions just described were contributory causes for Swedish immigration to America. However, the great majority of the Swedes left their homeland because they were poor. There was no opportunity for them to better those conditions as long as they remained in Sweden.

Advertisement to attract Swedish settlers to Minnesota.

3000 LABORERS
WANTED
On the *LAKE SUPERIOR AND MISSISSIPPI RAILROAD from Duluth at the Western Extremity of Lake Superior, to ST. PAUL*

Constant Employment will be given.   Wages range from $2.00 to $4.00 per Day.

MECHANICS
Are Needed at Duluth!
Wages to Masons and Plasterers, $4.00 per day; Carpenters, $3.00 per day.

10,000 EMIGRANTS
WANTED TO SETTLE ON THE LANDS OF THE COMPANY, NOW OFFERED ON LIBERAL CREDITS AND AT LOW PRICES.

Large bodies of Government Lands, subject to *Homestead* Settlement, or open to *Pre-Emption.* These Lands offer Facilities to Settlers not surpassed, if equalled by any lands in the West. They lie *right along the line* of the Railroad connecting Lake Superior with the Mississippi River, one of the most important Roads in the West. Forty miles of the Road are now in running order, and the whole Road (150 miles) will be completed by June, 1870. WHITE and YELLOW PINE, and VALUABLE HARDWOOD, convenient to Market, abound.

The SOIL is admirably adapted to the raising of WINTER WHEAT and TAME GRASSES. *Stock have Good Pasture until the Depth of Winter.*

The waters of Lake Superior, in connection with the Timber, make this much the warmest part of Minnesota. The navigation season at Duluth is several weeks longer than on the Mississippi. The LUMBER interest will furnish abundant and profitable *WINTER WORK.*

FREE TRANSPORTATION over the completed portion of the Railroad will be given to Laborers and all Settling on the Lands of the Company.

At Duluth *Emigrants* and their families will find *free* quarters in a new and commodious *Emigrant House,* until they locate themselves, by applying at Duluth to LUKE MARVIN, Agent. *Laborers* will report to WM. BRANCH, Contractor of the Road. For information as to Steamers to Duluth, inquire at Transportation Office in any of the Lake Cities.

DULUTH, MINN., JUNE 14, 1869.   "DULUTH MINNESOTIAN" PRINT.

2. *Advantages in America*

Ever since the founding of the first English colonies America has been a place where the poor, the oppressed, the rich, the educated, and the uneducated could come and find new and better ways of living. Regardless of nationality or creed, America from the first offered opportunities for a better life for those who were willing to take those opportunities. It was quite natural then that the people in Sweden should want at this time to come to the United States.

What were some of the opportunities and advantages offered to immigrants? First of all there was much fertile land. There were millions of acres of land that could be purchased for a few dollars per acre. In 1862 the Congress passed the Homestead Act. By this law the United States Government promised to give 160 acres of land to any adult who was 21 years of age if he would live on it and improve it for five years. At the end of five years all the government charged was a small fee for passing the deed, or title to the land, to the owner. Most of this land was in the Middle West.

The climate in the Middle Western States was suitable for growing a great variety of crops. The yield per acre was far greater than any the immigrants had ever known. All the newcomer needed to do on the prairie was turn over the sod and plant the seeds for his crops.

The forest regions in the Great Lakes area attracted many of the Swedes. The lakes, streams, and timber were much like their native land. The timber could be used for building homes. The forests, lakes and streams supplied fish and wild game. To the poor peasants this seemed like paradise.

Land companies and railroad companies were eager for settlers. They offered not only cheap land and many opportunities for farming, but also transportation from Europe to America. Many land companies wanted the Scandinavians as settlers.

Laborers received higher wages and the standard of living in the United States was higher. Letters sent to friends and relatives in Sweden painted glowing pictures of unusual opportunities in America.

Religious freedom was granted to all persons. There was no restriction on the type of religious belief or the form of religious worship. Everyone could worship where, when, and how he pleased.

Every immigrant coming to the United States was eligible to vote as soon as he was naturalized and 21 years of age. In some states he could vote as soon as he received his first citizenship papers. The great majority of Swedish immigrants eagerly awaited the opportunity to vote and take part in local government.

There was no class distinction in America. There were no titled noblemen and women and no aristocracy such as the immigrants had known in Sweden.

When the people of Sweden learned about all the advantages and opportunities that could be found in America it is not surprising that they came by the thousands to seek new homes in this land of plenty.

3. *Immigration to the North Central States*

During the middle of the 19th century, when the mass immigration of Swedish people to the United States began, the majority came to the North Central States. The greatest number of the Swedish immigrants settled in Illinois, Minnesota, Iowa, Kansas, and Nebraska. This was due to the thousands of acres of govern-

Sod house, a typical immigrant home on the Minnesota prairie.

Immigrant party of Swedes on their way to the Middle West.

IMMIGRANT PARTY OF SWEDES.

ment land in those states which could be purchased at a very low price. After the Homestead Act was passed much land could be obtained for practically no money.

The Swedish people who came at this period in our history were land-conscious. They believed firmly that land ownership guaranteed not only a high standard of living but also a good social standing. This desire for land was an important factor in building up rural communities in Illinois, Minnesota, Iowa, and Kansas.

Practically all the immigrants to the Middle West came from New York by way of the Erie Canal and the Great Lakes to Chicago. This stopping place became a gateway to the rich farming lands in the upper Mississippi River Valley. Here the Swedish immigrants would be met by land agents who directed them farther west. However, many of the newcomers stayed in Chicago. Work was plentiful for even at that early date Chicago was becoming a great industrial and trading center. For that reason Chicago has always had a large Swedish population. The United States Census for 1960 gives the number of Swedes living in Chicago, but born in Sweden, as 26,316.

Minneapolis, Minnesota, is another city which has a large population of people who were born in Sweden, as do many other cities in the Middle West. More than half of the first generation of Swedes in America live in the 11 North Central States.

Dormitory-style building of 196 rooms where the people of the Bishop Hill Colony lived, 1846.

Church built by the Janssonites in the Bishop Hill Colony, 1848.

Many of the Swedish immigrants came over to America in groups and settled together in a community. There were advantages in doing this. They were able to share their material goods and also the hardships, sacrifices, and toil they had to endure. Later they shared their achievements, too.

Although the majority of the immigrants came for land and became farmers, there were some who came for religious freedom. One such group settled at Bishop Hill, Illinois. This settlement was composed of the Swedish followers of Eric Jansson, a lay preacher in Northern Sweden. He had broken with the State Church, denounced its clergy, burned the books of Martin Luther, and forbidden his followers to have any contact with the established religion. For this he had been arrested and put in jail. However, he managed to get released and decided to leave Sweden. He induced his followers to sell their property and put their money into a common treasury preparatory to leaving for America.

One of the Jansson followers, Olaf Olsson, with his wife, two children and two associates, was sent to America in 1845. He was instructed to buy a large tract of land suitable for the founding of a religious colony. Olsson went to western Illinois where land was plentiful, fertile, and cheap. He purchased a large area for $1.25 per acre.

In the fall of 1846 Eric Jansson and a group of settlers joined Olaf Olsson in western Illinois and founded a colony which they named Bishop Hill after Jansson's hometown in Sweden.

During the first winter the Janssonites lived in caves dug out of a hillside. There was much sickness and many deaths. Later arrivals brought the Asiatic Cholera to the colony which caused many more deaths. Jansson's own wife became one of the victims of the plague. Jansson held absolute rule over his followers. All property was owned in common, and the people lived together in large, brick dormitory-style buildings. Some of these are still standing. So is the Colony Church and the Steeple Building which contains a remarkable four-faced town clock that still runs. In the Colony Church, where Jansson preached, may still be seen the

Schoolhouse in
Bishop Hill Colony, 1860.

original benches of finely carved walnut. Here, too, is a remarkable art gallery containing a large collection of paintings of the leaders of the colony, done by the self-taught artist Olaf Krantz. The collection is now very valuable for it represents one of the few examples of early American art.

After the first years of hardship the colony began to prosper. The soil in this section of Illinois was rich and the people were thrifty and industrious. They had their own sawmill and flour mill, and they made their own bricks for their buildings. In the fields, barns, and shops the people worked with military precision. In a few years they owned 8,500 acres of land, of which 3,350 acres were under cultivation. They also had 200 milk cows, 600 additional cattle, and 50 yoke of oxen. They manufactured brooms from broomcorn and linen from flax, which in 1854 brought in about $36,000. This modern Utopia did not last long, for less than four years after the colony was founded Jansson was killed.

John Root, a former sergeant in the Swedish army, had married Jansson's cousin. When he tried to take her away from the colony, Jansson refused to let her go. She was the victim of a series of kidnappings by both sides, and finally both Jansson and Root were summoned to appear in the county courthouse at Cambridge. When Root walked into the courtroom he shot Jansson who died immediately. Jansson's followers expected him to rise again on the third day, but when nothing happened they buried him in the colony cemetery. This was the beginning of the end of the colony although it was not dissolved until 1860. Having no strong leader to take the place of Jansson after his death, the colony was incorporated as a company and seven men were chosen to be the directors. There was much rivalry as to who should take over as the successor to Jansson. Mismanagement plunged the colony into debt amounting to about $700,000. After this happened the members decided to divide the property and dissolve the corporation.

As a religious group, the Janssonite movement disappeared. Some of the people joined the Seventh-Day Adventists, others joined the Swedenborgians, but the largest number became members of the Methodist Church, which is the only church in Bishop Hill today. Many abandoned religion completely. Bishop Hill is now a state park and the old colony church is a museum instead of a house of worship. Nevertheless, the monument in the village park states that its founders left Sweden to escape persecution and to find religious freedom in the New World.

In the same year that the Bishop Hill Colony was founded another group of Swedish immigrants settled in New Sweden, Iowa. This was on the other side of the Mississippi River, not many miles away. They did not have a self-appointed spiritual leader as did the Janssonites. They were Lutherans and had not broken away from the State Church in Sweden. Their chief purpose for coming to America was land and better opportunities for themselves and their children. A humble blacksmith by the name of M. F. Hokanson was their pastor.

Aerial photo of Bishop Hill, Illinois, today. In the park stands a monument with an inscription, written in both Swedish and English, that reads:
Dedicated to the Memory of the Hardy Pioneers,
Who, in Order to Secure Religious Liberty, Left
Sweden, Their Native Land with all the Endearments
of Home and Kindred, and Founded Bishop Hill Colony
on the Uninhabited Prairies of Illinois.

27

U.S. postage stamp commemorating the 100th anniversary of the coming of Swedish settlers to the Middle West.

Not more than ten miles from Bishop Hill is the village of Andover, Illinois. This place was settled by another group of Swedish immigrants. Their leader was the Rev. Lars P. Esbjorn, a Lutheran minister from Sweden, who preached the gospel and founded the first Swedish Lutheran church in the Middle West.

New Sweden and Andover are two communities settled for homes and land, yet they became the two cradles of the Augustana Lutheran Church Synod in America. The spiritual influence of the people and their leaders, Hokanson and Esbjorn, became known to the Swedish people in all parts of the United States. Thousands of Lutheran congregations were organized as a result of the faith and leadership in those two pioneer farming communities.

Shortly after the Civil War another famous Swedish community was founded. It was the last of the Swedish mass settlements in the Middle West. In April 1868, a group of recently arrived immigrants in Chicago under the leadership of Sven A. Lindell organized a company which was called the "The First Swedish Agricultural Company." The purpose of this group was to acquire suitable land in the Middle West and establish a Swedish Lutheran Colony. The company purchased 13,160 acres of land in the Smoky River Valley of central Kansas. The price was $2.25 per acre.

After the land had been purchased the first problem was to get settlers who could buy portions of the land and make productive farms. The company's terms specified that each person who became a member had to be a believing Christian, follow the teachings of the Swedish Lutheran Church, be industrious, and help the community and the company in its growth. The new settlement was to be called "Lindsborg" in honor of the three principal founders, Sven Lindell, S. P. Lindgren and Daniel Lindahl.

The first group of immigrants arrived in the summer of 1869. There were about 250 persons, including children. Their leader was a young Lutheran preacher by the name of Olaf Olsson. He had objected to some of the teachings of the State Church, which had displeased the Bishop of Sweden.

At Lindsborg the newcomers experienced the same hardships that all the pioneers had to endure. However, they managed to survive and by Christmas 1870 they had built a little stone church as their place of worship.

More settlers came later but, as only true believers of the Lutheran Church could settle in the community and everyone had to pass a test before the elders of the church, dissension arose and the settlers disagreed and quarreled with the founders of the company. Finally the company was dissolved and this Utopia, like the one at Bishop Hill, came to an end. The community of Lindsborg, however, became famous as an education and music center. In 1879 Rev. Carl Swensson, a newly ordained pastor, succeeded Rev. Olaf Olsson, the leader of the original settlers. Under Rev. Swensson's leadership Bethany College was built. It was he and his wife who organized the Lindsborg Oratorio Chorus, which has become quite famous.

4. *Immigration to Other Sections of the United States*

Swedish immigration was never very heavy in the New England States. The soil was poor and as the immigrants wanted good farming land there was no inducement to settle in that region.

The cities in New England, however, attracted skilled craftsmen who had learned to work with copper, brass, silver, and other metals.

In the 1800's a group of Swedes was brought over to settle in northern Maine. The population here was declining and the State

Commissioner of Immigration was eager to reverse this trend with farmers from Sweden. About 114 immigrants came in 1870. They settled in the Aroostook potato district. Ten years later the number in the colony was 787. Shortly after this the state of Maine leased its forest lands to private lumber companies so there was no more free land for the immigrants. That put an end to Swedish immigration to Maine.

After the Delaware colony was lost there was very little emigration from Sweden to the English colonies. However, when the masses of Swedes came over after the Civil War many stayed in New York. Those who were interested in farming went to western New York State. The city of Jamestown in that area has a large Swedish population.

Metalworking and other technical industries drew some Swedes to the seaboard and industrial cities in the Middle Atlantic States. The number who came, however, was not large.

The South did not attract Swedish immigrants. The climate was much too different from that of Sweden. The forests were different and there were few lakes. Then, too, slavery was objectionable to the Swedes. One exception, however, was an early and influential settlement around Austin, Texas. The leader was a Swedish immigrant by the name of Sven Svenson. This community was important in the development of Texas.

A few immigrants found their way into the Mountain States. They settled in the forested areas of Montana, Wyoming, and Idaho. Others went to the mining areas around Denver, Colorado, and Butte, Montana.

The gold rush of 1849-1850 lured many of the Swedes to seek their fortunes in the mines of California. According to the Census of 1960, California has about the same number of Swedes as Minnesota. They are concentrated in the cities.

Forests, lumbering, and fishing attracted the Swedes to settle in Oregon and Washington. Most of them settled in the Middle West first and then moved to the Pacific Northwest. The Swedish population is about evenly distributed between the urban and the rural areas in that region.

5. *High and Low Points in Immigration*

Sweden, with a population of about six million, lost one million people through immigration during the last half of the 19th century and the first half of the 20th century. This was a period of 100 years. Most of those emigrants came to the United States.

During the periods of heaviest emigration, one out of every seven persons left Sweden. Some of the provinces in the central and northern parts of the country were almost depopulated of young men and women of the lower and middle classes of people.

Between the years 1816 and 1850 about 9,561 Swedes came to America. Immigration increased in the 1850's until it averaged about 1,690 annually. During the ten years from 1861 to 1870 the number was 12,245 annually. Immigration then increased greatly until it reached 39,000 in 1880, 49,000 in 1881, and 64,000 in 1882. This latter figure was the largest number that came over in any one year. The next highest was 54,000 in 1888.

Young Scandinavian woman immigrant dressed in her native costume.

Swedish Immigration to the United States by Decades

DECADE	NUMBER OF IMMIGRANTS
1851-1860	16,900
1861-1870	122,447
1871-1880	150,269
1881-1890	376,401
1891-1900	246,772
1901-1910	257,670
1911-1920	118,370
1921-1930	97,317
1931-1940	2,511
1941-1950	8,379
1951-1960	18,714
1961-1964	7,520

States Having Largest Number of People Born in Sweden (1960 Census)

Illinois	34,606
California	26,553
Minnesota	25,323
New York	23,516
Massachusetts	13,607
Washington	13,507

Cities Having Largest Number of People Born in Sweden (1960 Census)

Chicago	26,316
New York	17,071
St. Paul — Minneapolis	13,114
Los Angeles — Long Beach	11,709
San Francisco — Oakland	6,902
Boston	6,526
Detroit	2,875
Philadelphia	1,632

By the year 1900 the number of foreign-born Swedes living in the United States was 500,000. In 1910 this number had increased to 600,000. After that date immigration diminished due to World War I which made traveling dangerous. In 1920 the United States passed immigration laws limiting the number of people who could come into our country each year.

The depression in the United States and in Europe during the 1930's caused another decline in immigration. The Second World War in the 1940's caused the number to drop to the lowest it has ever been. Only 57 Swedish immigrants came to the United States in 1945.

Nineteenth century Swedish immigrants on their way to America are shown in the painting *Foredeck During Storm* by Knut Ekwall.

PART III.

Swedish Contributions to American Life

1. *Agriculture*

The first contributions by the Swedes to American agriculture were in the colony of New Sweden on the Delaware River. Although this colony was founded to trade for fur and tobacco with the Indians, the first settlers realized very early that the success of the colony would depend upon agriculture.

Large tracts of land were purchased from the Indians and Governor Johan Printz urged the settlers to produce good breeds of cattle and sheep. The natural meadows along the river furnished pasture and hay crops for the livestock. Rye, Indian corn, and barley were the crops grown for food. Flax was grown for hemp because flax and wool were the raw materials used in making clothing. Tobacco was grown for export to Europe. Traces of the Swedish influence in agriculture can still be found in the type of farm buildings and red cattle one sees in Delaware and Pennsylvania.

When mass emigration from Sweden began in the 1860's the majority of the emigrants were farmers. Those farmers and their descendants have played an important part in the development of agriculture in the Middle West and Pacific Coast states. They built thousands of homes and turned millions of acres of virgin land into farms.

An immigrant home in western Minnesota about 1880.

The first Swedish settlers in Minnesota chose the wooded areas for their farms. They did this because that was the type of land they had lived on in Sweden. Then, too, it was a common belief among all newcomers to America that forest-covered lands had the richest soil. If no trees grew on the land the soil would be poor. The timber on the land was needed for building houses. It was also used for fuel. However, the clearing of the land was slow and it was hard work to get enough open space for growing crops. Therefore many early settlers were soon convinced that the open prairies made better farms. All they needed to do there was plow the land and plant the seeds for the soil was richer and deeper than the wooded lands.

It is difficult to single out any individual farmer or group of farmers who have made outstanding contributions to American agriculture. The Swedish farmers have contributed much toward community cooperation and neighborliness. They were always ready to aid, comfort, and cheer each other in times of sickness, death, and misfortune. When new settlers arrived in the community they were given food and shelter until they could build their own homes. Help was given in erecting the farm buildings. Machinery and tools were loaned to the newcomer so he could plant his crops. During harvesting and threshing the neighbors helped each other until the work was finished. This spirit of cooperation and sharing has been handed down to the present generation and is typical of most of our rural communities.

The Swedish farmers practiced diversified farming. This was necessary for the farm had to produce food and shelter for the family and the livestock. In some communities raw materials for clothing, such as flax and wool, also had to be produced.

The Scandinavian immigrants, the Swedes, Danes and Norwegians, very early developed cooperatives. When they found it difficult to market farm products they started their marketing cooperatives. When they saw the need for buying consumer goods at a lower price, they organized consumer cooperatives. Today the Scandinavians and the Finns are very active in promoting cooperatives.

The farmers of Swedish descent are recognized among the better farmers of their respective communities. In some states, Minnesota in particular, where Master-Farmer awards have been given the best farmers, those of Swedish descent have received a large percentage of the awards.

Alsike clover, an important forage crop, was first introduced in the United States by the Swedish farmers. Victory oats, which is a popular and high yielding variety, came from a plant breeding station in a village in southern Sweden. Hannchen barley was also introduced in America from that same plant breeding station. It has proven to be one of our best yielding varieties.

In scientific forestry the Swedes have taught us how to study forest soils, to take inventories of our forest resources and to use methods of reforestation. Many forestry specialists from the United States have gone to Sweden to study their methods of forest conservation. Among these was Gen. Christopher Andrews who as United States Minister to Sweden learned what that country was doing to preserve its forests. On his return to the United States he urged both the national and state governments to develop similar conservation methods. That was the beginning of our forest conservation on a state and a national scale.

Several inventions by Swedes have been very beneficial to the agriculture industry. The cream separator invented by Carl G. DeLaval in 1877 was an important event to the dairy industry. He invented both the power-driven and the hand separators which have been so widely used in America. He also invented the first practical milk tester. It was this invention that helped Stephen Babcock to invent the Babcock tester, which is used to test the amount of butterfat in milk. Other inventions by DeLaval are the centrifugal churn and one of the first milking machines.

The Swedes succeeded as farmers in America for life in Sweden had accustomed them to hardships. Experience had taught them to be thrifty, industrious, frugal, and patient. They were quick to adapt themselves to their new environment. They became naturalized citizens as soon as it was legally possible for them to do so. The Swedish farmer felt the need to become a citizen so he could help make the laws which would benefit him and the community in which he lived.

2. *Business, Trade, Manufacturing*

The Swedes could not have existed long in the severe climate of their country if they had not been resourceful. It is the surface of the land, the climate, and the natural resources of a country that mold people. The Swedes were especially fitted to make their living in the northern and central parts of the United States.

In the early years the Swedes, like the other north European people who came to America, were farmers. They got along with the simplest equipment they could make themselves, unless they were able to bring some from Europe. As American industries developed, the Swedes took their place in industry and in business as craftsmen, organizers, and executives.

We need to remember that although the immigrants were poorly supplied with goods when they came to America, they did know how to make the tools necessary for tilling the soil and for building houses. Among each group that came there were tailors, shoemakers, blacksmiths, carpenters, cabinetmakers, stone-masons, bricklayers, and other craftsmen. With the abundance of raw materials which they found in America, the Swedes were prepared not only to take care of themselves but also to provide others with both handmade and machine-made goods. As a rule they preferred to work in wood or metal for these were the raw materials they had worked with in Sweden.

The first trading which the Swedes did in America was with the Indians in the colony of New Sweden. Jonas Nilsson, who came over with Governor Printz, established a trading post in what is now the city of Philadelphia. He built up an extensive and profitable trade with the Indians in that region.

In the year 1838 Sven Svenson, a young clerk from Sweden, was shipwrecked off the coast of Texas near Galveston. He went from Galveston to Austin where he obtained work as a clerk in a general store. After working for a few years he became the owner of a large store in Austin. Later he went into the hotel and the banking business. After the Civil War he started a cotton export business in New Orleans. Disposing of that business, he moved to New York City where he founded an important banking house. His descendants are important in banking in New York today. It was due to the efforts of Sven Svenson that many Swedes came to Texas in the 1850's.

Chicago attracted many Swedes who later became businessmen in that city. One of these was Robert Lindblom. He became a well-known civic leader, a member of the Chicago Board of Trade, the Board of Education, and other civic organizations. A city high school was named for him. Another prominent civic leader was Charles Peterson, the owner of a large printing company. He, too, was a member of the Board of Education, the City Board of Finance, the Swedish Club, the Swedish Choral Society and at one time he was the treasurer of the city of Chicago.

Edgar Mattson, the son of Hans Mattson who was so influential in bringing Swedish settlers to Minnesota, became a well-

Charles R. Walgreen, founder
of the Walgreen Drug Stores.

First Walgreen drug store.

known banker. At the age of 19 he was a bank messenger. From
that position he advanced until he became president of the bank.
Today that bank is the Midland National Bank and Trust Company.

Some Swedes have attained prominence in general merchandising. One of the best known in this occupation is Walter Hoving.
He first worked with the R. H. Macy department store in New
York City and became its executive vice-president. From Macy's
he went to Chicago and became vice-president of Montgomery
Ward and Company. In 1936 he left Chicago and returned to New
York. In 1937 he became president of Lord and Taylor, a prominent
store on Fifth Avenue. Today he is the chairman of Tiffany & Co.

The name of Walgreen is quite familiar to the people of the
United States. Charles Walgreen, the founder of this nationwide

Charles R. Walgreen, Jr. son of
the founder and chairman of the
board.

A modern Walgreen drug store, Chicago, Illinois.

chain of drug stores, was born near Galesburg, Illinois, in 1873 of Swedish parents. He began by working in a shoe factory. While there he injured one of his hands and had to quit. His doctor persuaded him to accept a job in a drug store. Although he was not familiar with chemicals and drugs, he took the job. In a short time he became interested in the business and management of the store. Through his interest in serving customers, his ambition, and his ability, he later opened his own drug store in Chicago in 1901. Mr. Walgreen soon opened another store, then many more, until today there are about 500 drug stores bearing the Walgreen name throughout the United States and Puerto Rico. Besides the stores, the company owns many warehouses, ice cream plants, and laboratories. Charles R. Walgreen, Jr., son of the founder, is chairman of the board.

Swedes have also made worthy contributions in transportation. A native-born Swede, William Matson, was the founder of the Matson Navigation Company. In the late 1800's he began carrying general merchandise to Hawaii and returning with raw sugar, pineapple, and coffee. From one small schooner he built up his

Mesabi Transportation Company buses, forerunner of the Greyhound Lines, 1918.

Carl Eric Wickman, Swedish immigrant and mine worker, founded the Greyhound Bus Lines in Hibbing, Minnesota.

trade so that today the company owns more than 38 freighters and a dozen luxury liners which carry freight and passengers from our cities on the west coast to Hawaii, Australia, and the islands of the Pacific Ocean.

The founder of the Greyhound Bus Line, Carl Eric Wickman, was born in Sweden and came to the United States at the age of 17. He worked in the iron mines at Hibbing, Minnesota, when he conceived the idea of a "jitney" or bus service transporting the miners to and from the mines. His first bus was a secondhand automobile. From this humble beginning the Greyhound Corporation was developed. It is now the largest bus company in the United States with buses operating from coast to coast, and in Canada and Mexico.

It is natural for the Swedish people to be interested in the growth of plants. Therefore we have many in the florist business. The first professional florist in the Middle West was P. S. Peterson who established the 500-acre Rose Hill Nursery near Chicago. He had a thriving business and made millions of dollars before he died.

Another Swede by the name of Peterson came to Connecticut in 1870. He had to borrow money to start his greenhouse. As his business grew he developed one of the largest greenhouses in the country, covering over one million square feet. Mr. Peterson became known as the Rose King of America, because he developed many new varieties of roses. The business is still owned and operated by his descendants.

John E. Lager, who had many greenhouses in New Jersey, specialized in growing orchids. He led several orchid hunting expeditions to South America in search for new varieties. On one of these expeditions he found a plant which produced pure white orchids. From this plant he grew an orchid which was sold for $10,000 to a European company.

Food production and distribution is another enterprise the Swedes have engaged in. C. A. Swanson and Sons of Omaha, Nebraska, are noted nationally for canned and frozen turkeys and chickens. Their frozen TV dinners and other frozen foods are found in every supermarket in the country.

Swedish restaurants are popular, particularly those specializing in "Smorgasbord," which is an extensive variety of dishes served buffet style, and where the diner is permitted to serve himself as often as he wishes. The buffet style originated in Sweden.

3. *Engineering, Science and Invention*

Engineering and invention are especially favored in a country like Sweden for the value of man and his services has always been highly regarded. Sweden has never allowed slavery or serfdom among its people. Furthermore, due to its climate, it has never been overpopulated.

Handicraft came naturally to the rural Swedish people. During the long winter months, when the days were very short, men were busy making many kinds of useful articles for the home, in addition to farm tools and implements. Spinning wheels, looms for weaving, implements for sowing and reaping, and hand or water driven mills for grinding grains were some of the implements which the people of Sweden had made for centuries.

Nature had provided the wood and the iron from which the implements were made. Then, too, there was plenty of waterpower. It was just a matter of harnessing that power for running the mills.

After 1880 Swedish engineers became known for their skill in all branches of industry in the United States. Today we find engineers of Swedish descent in practically every large manufacturing plant. We also find them as designers of all kinds of power development plants and equipment.

The earliest Swedish engineer to make a great contribution to the United States was John Ericsson. He designed and built the *Monitor,* one of the first ironclad battleships. Ericsson is no doubt the best known and most honored Swedish-American engineer, not only for his inventions but also for his service at a time when it was needed so much. The victory of the *Monitor* over the *Merrimac* during the Civil War saved the Union navy and helped win the war for the North. As an inventor, John Ericsson's accomplishments were many. He patented more than 100 items, including the screw propeller.

A U.S. postage stamp honoring John Ericsson, builder of the *Monitor,* was issued in connection with the unveiling of his monument in 1926. Notice the shields of the U.S. and Sweden in the upper corners.

John Ericsson, designer and builder of the *Monitor,* the first ironclad warship in the U.S. Navy.

The battle between the ironclad warships, *Merrimac* and *Monitor*, during the Civil War, 1862.

The firm of Stromberg and Carlson is very familiar to the American public. Both men were born in Sweden. They originally made telephones and burglar alarms. More recently they have manufactured radios and television sets. John Gullborg invented a carburetor known as the Stromberg Carburetor. At the time of his invention he was employed by Stromberg and Carlson. Gullborg also invented the grease gun for lubricating automobiles.

Gustaf Kallberg, associated for many years with the Allis Chalmers Company, designed large pumping engines for municipal waterworks. He also invented high-pressure pumps which are used for pumping oil through pipelines from the oil fields to refineries and from the refineries to customers.

One of our best known inventors is Vincent Bendix. He invented the Bendix self-starter which has been installed in millions

Alfred Stromberg organized a company for making telephones and burglar alarms.

Andrew Carlson, a partner of Alfred Stromberg in the manufacture of radios and electrical equipment.

Stromberg and Carlson radio and television manufacturing plant in Rochester, New York.

of cars. Later he invented a carburetor, four-wheel brakes, and the Bendix automatic washing machine. After Charles Lindbergh's successful flight to Paris, Mr. Bendix became interested in aviation. He acquired several companies manufacturing instruments for airplanes and created the Bendix Aviation Corporation.

Another great name in the field of invention is Dr. Ernst F. W. Alexanderson. He was born in Sweden and received his education in electrical and mechanical engineering at the Royal Technical University in Stockholm. Coming to the United States in 1901 he worked with the C & C Electric Company in New Jersey. A few years later, he joined the General Electric Company at Schenectady, New York. His biographers credit him with giving radio to America. General Electric regards him as their most prolific inventor. He holds 315 patents and he averaged one every seven

Vincent Bendix, inventor of the Bendix automatic washing machine and the self-starter for automobiles.

Dr. Ernst F. W. Alexanderson, inventor of the radio receiver, cascade tuning, and transmitter modulation.

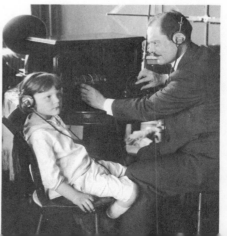

45

Thomas J. Watson, Jr., Chairman of the Board of the International Business Machines Corporation, New York.

Dr. Glenn Seaborg, winner of the 1951 Nobel prize in chemistry and Chairman of the U.S. Atomic Energy Commission.

weeks during the 46 years he worked for General Electric.

Dr. Alexanderson has made contributions to guiding systems for aircraft, the automatic steering of aircraft and watercraft, and of ways to determine altitude from aircraft. His inventions are too numerous to list and he has received many awards for his accomplishments.

Other inventors include Sven R. Bergman, also with General Electric, who invented the high-speed rayon spinning bucket and Gideon Sundback, who invented the zipper fastener.

Among the most important firms in the world today in the highly technical field of computers and automation is the International Business Machines Corporation, of which Thomas J. Watson, Jr. is chairman. Mr. Watson is of Swedish parentage. Besides his prominence in the world of business and industry he is also a trustee of the Rockefeller Foundation, a director of Time Incorporated, and a member of the National Executive Board of the Boy Scouts of America.

There are a number of prominent American scientists of Swedish descent. One who is very well-known is Dr. Glenn T. Seaborg, chairman of the Atomic Energy Commission. Dr. Seaborg was born in Michigan of Swedish parents. At the age of 10 the family moved to California. Here he received his education. As a professor of chemistry at the University of California at Berkeley in 1940, he and his co-workers discovered plutonium and other elements such as uranium isotopes and the isotope of neptunium. He was the winner of the Nobel prize in chemistry in 1951.

Dr. Carl D. Anderson is one of the most famous of all American nuclear physicists. He was born in New York City of Swedish parents. For several years he has been connected with the California Institute of Technology. In 1936 he won the Nobel prize in physics for his discovery of the positron.

The field of aviation is so closely related to engineering that it is advisable to include it in this chapter. We know that the Scandinavians have been a seafaring people as far back as history has any record of the Norsemen. The skill and daring of the Vikings at sea has been told in prose, poetry, and song. Therefore it was natural for the people in Sweden and the Swedes in America to become interested in aviation. The Swedes have made important contributions in flying, in designing, in constructing, and in servicing all types of aircraft. They are important in operating various airlines.

The first Swede to become well-known in aviation was Major Erik Nelson. In 1921, he was one of the engineers on the first flight from New York to Nome, Alaska. Three years later, in 1924, he was one of the pilots on an army plane that made the first flight around the world. That was three years before Charles A. Lindbergh's flight to Paris.

Before those two historic events, Major Nelson had been an instructor in flying for the United States Army. In 1928 he resigned from the army and became sales manager for Boeing Aircraft Company in Seattle. He remained with that company until his retirement in 1936.

Philip G. Johnson, another young engineer of Swedish descent, joined the Boeing Aircraft Company in 1917 as soon as he had graduated from the University of Washington. He began work in the production department and within 10 years he became the president of the company. In addition to his work with Boeing,

Philip G. Johnson, former president of Boeing Aircraft and co-founder of United Airlines and Trans-Canada Airlines.

Philip Johnson helped establish several air transport companies. Among these were United Airlines and Trans-Canada Airlines.

No one has been more prominent in aviation history than Charles A. Lindbergh, Jr. Perhaps no one up to the present time has received more awards for contributions in this field. After finishing his training in the United States Army Air Corps he was the pilot on a plane carrying mail between Chicago and St. Louis. It was at this time that he decided to try for the $35,000 prize offered to anyone who would make the first nonstop flight between New York and Paris. The result of that successful flight is well known by people the world over. The event was not only the beginning of air transportation between the United States and Europe but it also made Charles Lindbergh a world hero.

Vice-Admiral Charles E. Rosendahl was an air specialist for the United States Navy in lighter-than-air dirigibles. After World War I he was an instructor at the Annapolis Naval Academy in the operation of large rigid dirigibles. He did more experimenting with this type of aircraft than any other American. At that time he felt that dirigibles were necessary for the defense of our country. Admiral Rosendahl wrote many magazine articles and books on dirigibles and their importance. Two of his most popular books are *Up Ship* and *What About Airships?*

Another important Swedish aviator was Martin E. Johnson. He became a famous naturalist, lecturer, and photographer of wildlife as well as a skilled pilot. He first became famous when he accompanied Mr. and Mrs. Jack London as a photographer on a voyage to the South Sea Islands. A few years later, under the sponsorship of the American Museum of Natural History, Johnson and his wife, Osa, flew around the world six times taking pictures of wild animal life in Africa, the East Indies and the islands of the Pacific Ocean. On these flights he piloted his own plane. His pictures, lectures, and books are known to thousands of Americans. In January 1937 Mr. Johnson was killed in an airplane crash in California. Mrs. Johnson survived the crash and has continued to carry on his work. Their most popular book is *Camera Trails in Africa*.

Charles Lindbergh, Jr. and *The Spirit of St. Louis,* in which plane he became the first man to fly alone across the Atlantic Ocean.

4. Education

Many of the very first Swedish immigrants who came to America could barely read. Not all of them could write. However, those who came after 1865 could read, write, and had some knowledge of arithmetic. Sweden had passed a compulsory education law about 1842. Public schools were built after that date so the law could be enforced.

In addition to reading, writing, and arithmetic the public schools taught Bible history and geography. Every child had to memorize Martin Luther's catechism and many hymns from the church hymn book. The pastor of each local parish supervised education, which was for the most part religious.

We have mentioned that the Swedes were quick to adopt American ways. This was true in education, too, for they valued education highly and made great sacrifices to provide schools for their children. After the pioneers had built homes for themselves they built a church and then took part in organizing public schools in their communities. The Swedish settlers were strongly in favor of a strict separation of church and state. They believed that the state, not the church, should provide public education.

In every community the church was their center for civic and social activities. Therefore, there was a need for training their ministers and preparatory schools, colleges, and seminaries were built. The preparatory schools were called academies. They prepared students for college, as our high schools do today. There were few public high schools in the United States until after the Civil War.

The first colleges founded by Swedes were established by those of the Lutheran faith. Rev. Tuve N. Hasselquist started classes in his home in Chicago in 1864. This was not satisfactory so the classes were moved to Paxton, Illinois. Finally, the newly organized Lutheran Synod of Northern Illinois bought a tract of land on the Mississippi River between Rock Island and Moline. Here a college was built and named Augustana College and Seminary. The first building was ready in 1875.

Through the years the college and seminary have grown and become recognized as an accredited institution of higher learning. In addition to training young men for the ministry, the college has paid considerable attention to the various fields in education, particularly science. Many of our prominent scientists had their first training at Augustana College. Some prominent professors in history, sociology, and political science are graduates of this college. The present enrollment is 1,380 students and 101 instructors.

The second oldest Swedish Lutheran college was founded in 1862 near Red Wing, Minnesota, as an academy. This one, too, was started by a minister, Rev. Eric Norelius. The following year the school was moved to East Union, Minnesota and named St. Ansgars Academy. Twelve years later it was moved to St. Peter, Minnesota and renamed Gustavus Adolphus College in honor of the Swedish king. The college has grown and prospered. Its campus has many beautiful buildings and it is particularly noted for its science and music departments. Among its alumni have been three Minnesota governors.

The president of Gustavus Adolphus College, Dr. Edgar Carlson, is recognized as one of the outstanding Lutheran scholars in America. He is the author of several books and has written many articles on theology and education. He is also prominent as a speaker on educational, civic, and religious questions.

Dr. Edgar Carlson, President of Gustavus Adolphus College at St. Peter, Minnesota, educator, lecturer, and author.

Kenbrook Hall, a girl's dormitory at Upsala College, East Orange, New Jersey.

Bethany College at Lindsborg, Kansas, was organized as an academy in 1881 by Rev. Carl Swensson, a Lutheran pastor. Ten years later the academy became an accredited college. It has gained a wide recognition through its art and music departments. Its annual Messiah Festival given by the college's Oratorio Chorus is well-known in the Middle West.

Upsala College located at East Orange, New Jersey, is the fourth and youngest college founded and supported by the Swedish Lutheran Church. This college, too, was moved twice before the present location was found in 1924. It is growing rapidly and at present has a larger enrollment than any of the other colleges, namely 1,775 students.

North Park College in Chicago is owned and controlled by the Evangelical Mission Covenant Church. It was organized in 1891 by the Rev. E. S. Skogsbergh as a training institution for preachers. Later it was moved to Chicago and is now a four-year liberal arts college. Associated with the college is a divinity school, an academy, and a school of music.

The same church group owns the Minnehaha Academy, a four-year coeducational high school in Minneapolis, Minnesota. This school emphasizes courses in Christianity, and also college preparatory, general, and business courses. Bible study and chapel attendance are required of all students. The enrollment is limited to between 450 and 500 and is open to students of all religious faiths.

Bethel College and Seminary in St. Paul, Minnesota was founded as an academy by the Swedish Baptist Church. In the 1870's Dr. John Edgren made several attempts to establish a Baptist Theological Seminary in Chicago. This was not too successful so the Seminary was merged with the academy in St. Paul. In 1947 it became a four-year liberal arts college and took its present name. It is coeducational, growing rapidly, and is recognized for its fine music department.

Educators of Swedish descent who have gained national prominence include Miss Agnes Samuelson, who was State Superintendent of Schools in Iowa for several years. In 1935 she became president of the National Education Association. In 1945 she was appointed Assistant Director of Public Relations in Education in the Department of Health, Education and Welfare.

C. G. Schulz was Assistant Commissioner for eight years, then Commissioner of Education for 10 years, in the State of Minnesota. During this time he exerted a great influence on the state's educational policies. His leadership was responsible for many improvements in Minnesota public education.

Two nationally known professors from the University of Iowa are Dr. Carl E. Seashore and Dr. E. F. Lindquist. Dr. Seashore, a professor of psychology, did much valuable research in his field, especially as it related to music. His books and articles have brought about many changes in methods of teaching in our public schools. Dr. Lindquist is recognized as an authority on achievement testing.

Dr. A. A. Stromberg, former professor of Scandinavian languages at the University of Minnesota, was well-known for his work. Other nationally known professors at the University of Minnesota were Dr. David Swenson, professor of philosophy, Dr. George Stephenson, professor of history and Dr. A. O. Christianson, professor of agriculture. Dr. Stephenson did considerable research work in Swedish immigration and is an authority on that

Dr. Carl Seashore of the University of Iowa, noted research professor in psychology.

Dr. E. F. Lindquist of the University of Iowa, a national authority on achievement testing.

subject. T. A. Erickson of the College of Agriculture in St. Paul, Minnesota was the founder of the 4-H Clubs in Minnesota. He was a leader in that work for 25 years.

Alexander P. Anderson, a chemistry professor at the University of Minnesota, made over 15,000 experiments with cereal grains and starch. Through those experiments he discovered a method of blowing up the grains by firing them from guns. That discovery gave us puffed wheat, puffed rice, and other breakfast cereals.

Dr. Anderson's daughter-in-law is Mrs. Eugenie Anderson of Red Wing, Minnesota, the former United States Ambassadress to Denmark and Bulgaria.

5. *Government and Politics*

The Swedes have always had a great respect for law. From the earliest times the primitive Germanic tribes formulated rules for living and saw that they were enforced. An early code on which the present Swedish laws are based reads as follows: "The law is made for the guidance of all, rich or poor, and to define right from wrong. The law shall be observed and respected, protect the poor, maintain the peace for the peaceable, awe and chastise the unruly. The land shall be ruled by law not by violence."

The first Swedish settlers in Delaware, as well as the masses who came to America later, had this respect for law and order. When Johan Printz was sent over to be the governor of New Sweden, he had a set of written instructions with him. These became the laws of the colony as long as it was under Swedish control.

After the colony passed into the hands of the Dutch governor, and later under English governors, the people were given much voice in local government. The descendants of those first Swedish colonists continued to be prominent in government. Many became lawmakers, judges and public officials.

John Morton, a descendant of one of the early settlers of Delaware, was a prominent lawyer in Philadelphia for many years. He was made a justice of the Supreme Court of Pennsylvania and served in that office from 1770 to 1774. He was elected a delegate to the First Continental Congress, which ratified the Declaration of Independence on July 4, 1776 and was one of the signers of that great document.

Another descendant of a Swedish settler in Delaware was Alexander Hanson, a lawyer from Annapolis, Maryland. He, too, was a member of the Continental Congress and served as its president in 1781. Later, when the colonies became the United States, he was elected to Congress and served in the House of Representatives and also in the Senate.

Five different members of the Bayard family of Delaware have been United States Senators to Congress from that state. Thomas F. Bayard, was Secretary of State during Grover Cleveland's first term as President of the United States.

John Lind came to Minnesota from Sweden as a child. He was one of the first graduates of Gustavus Adolphus College at St. Peter. Later he attended the University of Minnesota where he studied law. He was elected to the United States Congress in 1886 and was re-elected twice. He was the first foreign-born Swede to serve in Congress. In 1898 he was elected governor of the State of Minnesota, and so became the first foreign-born Swede to serve as the governor of a state.

Another famous governor of Minnesota was John A. Johnson. He was born in St. Peter of Swedish parents. He was elected governor of Minnesota in 1906, served two years and was re-elected in 1908. However, he died suddenly in 1909 and did not serve out his second term. He was highly respected and loved by both political parties. His untimely death prevented him from being a candidate for the presidency of the United States.

Adolph O. Eberhart, a lawyer and an early graduate of Gustavus Adolphus College, succeeded Governor John A. Johnson. He, too, was born in Sweden and came to America as an immigrant. He was elected governor of Minnesota twice. Altogether Minnesota has had seven governors of Swedish parentage.

In addition to governors, Minnesota has had and still has many representatives in Congress of Swedish descent. Among these was Ernest Lundeen who served from 1917 to 1940. He became known nationally for his speeches condemning the corrupt practices of large trusts and corporations.

Charles A. Lindbergh, Sr., the father of Charles A. Lindbergh, the famous aviator, was elected to the House of Representatives in 1906. He was re-elected four times. It was he who started the famous investigation of the "money trusts." He was much opposed to the United States entrance in World War I. In 1919 he wrote a book entitled *Why Is Your Country at War?*

One of our outstanding government officials at the present time is Chief Justice of the United States Supreme Court Earl Warren. His mother was Swedish and his father Norwegian. Justice Warren was governor of California before his appointment as Chief Justice.

Another well-known person is Judge Luther Youngdahl. He was governor of Minnesota from 1947 to 1951. While governor he started reforms in the treatment of people in mental and correctional institutions of the state. At present he is a United States District Judge in Washington, D.C.

Charles A. Lindbergh, Sr. was a prominent U.S. Congressman from Minnesota who served from 1906-1914. He was the father of the famous aviator, who is seen here as a boy.

Earl Warren, Chief Justice of the U.S. Supreme Court, administering the oath of office to President John F. Kennedy. Five prominent immigrant groups are represented here: (from the left) Mrs. Jacqueline Bouvier Kennedy (French); former President Dwight D. Eisenhower (German); the Chief Justice (Swedish); President Kennedy (Irish); the then Vice-President Lyndon B. Johnson (English-Scotch-Irish). Former Vice-President Richard Nixon is shown on the far right.

A former governor of Minnesota who is nationally known is Orville Freeman. He was born and educated in Minneapolis and practiced law in that city until he was elected governor of the state in 1955. He served three terms in that office. When the late John F. Kennedy became President of the United States he appointed Orville Freeman Secretary of Agriculture, a position he retained in the administration of Lyndon Johnson.

Luther Youngdahl, U.S. District Judge in Washington, D.C., and former governor of Minnesota.

Orville Freeman, Secretary of Agriculture in the cabinets of Presidents Kennedy and Johnson, and former governor of Minnesota.

Clinton P. Anderson, U.S. Senator from New Mexico; Chairman of the Senate Committee on Aeronautical and Space Sciences.

Warren G. Magnusson, U.S. Senator from the State of Washington, who has served in the Senate for more than 18 years.

The first American of first-generation Swedish ancestry to be appointed to a post in the President's Cabinet is Clinton P. Anderson of Albuquerque, New Mexico. He was born in South Dakota but moved to New Mexico with his parents as a child and has lived there since. He became interested in politics at an early age. His first political job was state treasurer. He then became a representative to Congress where he served for several years. At the close of World War II he became United States Food Administrator. A few years later he was appointed Secretary of Agriculture in President Truman's Cabinet. He held that post until 1948 when he was elected United States Senator from New Mexico. He is serving his third term in the U.S. Senate, where he is a prominent member of several committees.

Another well-known member of the U.S. Senate is Warren G. Magnusson from the State of Washington. He was born in Minnesota of Swedish parents, and studied law at the University of Washington. He was a member of the Washington State Legislature for a few years and then appointed Assistant U.S. District Attorney. In 1937 he was elected Representative to the U.S. Congress and held that post until 1944, when he was appointed a U.S. Senator from his state. He is now serving his fourth term in the Senate and is one of its senior members.

Another Swede active in government is Frank Carlson of Concordia, Kansas. He was first elected as a representative to the

Frank Carlson, former U. S. Senator and governor from Kansas.

Admiral Arleigh Burke, former Chief of Naval Operations, U.S. Navy.

U.S. Congress in 1934 and was re-elected five times. In 1946 he was elected governor of Kansas and served two terms in that office. As governor he sponsored many reforms in his state's government. He served three terms as a U.S. Senator from Kansas and was an outstanding Republican in the Senate.

A very remarkable political career was made by Mary Anderson. She was born in Sweden and came to America at the age of 16. She first worked as a maid, then in a shoe factory. During that time she educated herself and became an important official in the shoemakers' union. She was appointed head of the Women's Bureau in the Department of Labor by President Wilson. She served in that capacity for 25 years and was instrumental in getting better working conditions and better wages for women factory workers.

Another woman active in government has been Esther Peterson. She was born in Utah of Swedish parents. After finishing college she taught school in Utah, and in Boston, Massachusetts. She has been legislative representative for the Industrial Union Department of the American Federation of Labor and the Congress of Industrial Organizations, Assistant Director of Labor Standards, Director of the Women's Bureau, and Assistant Secretary of Labor.

The Swedes have contributed some outstanding figures to the armed forces of the United States. One who has been prominent in recent times is Admiral Arleigh A. Burke, U.S.N., the retired

Chief of Naval Operations. He was born in Boulder, Colorado of Swedish parents. After graduating from the United States Naval Academy and the University of Michigan he entered the U.S. Navy and made that his career. During World War II he was chief of the Atlantic Fleet. At the outbreak of the Korean War he had charge of the Destroyer Force in the Pacific Ocean. In 1955 he was made Admiral and Chief of United States Naval Operations, at which post he remained until retirement in 1961. He has been given seven honorary degrees from different colleges and universities for his contributions to our armed services.

6. *Literature and the Press*

The foreign language press has had much influence on the Americanization of immigrants and did much work that the English language press could not do. The Swedish-American press was a good influence for improving the Swedish-born population in the United States. It advocated the welfare of the United States in times of war as well as in times of peace. It prepared the immigrants for their duties as American citizens. It tried to instruct its readers both as Swedes and as Americans. It tried to help the immigrants become good citizens as soon as possible. The press emphasized that in fostering a love for one's adopted country, the love for the mother country and its culture need not be lost. It stressed that the culture of a people is measured best by its educational system and by its literature and the press.

The earliest Swedish publications were of a religious order. The first Swedish paper, *Skandinaven*, was published in New York weekly from 1851 to 1853. The real beginning of a Swedish press was *Hemlandet* (Homeland). It was published in Galesburg, Illinois. The founder and editor was Rev. T. N. Hasselquist, the same energetic individual who founded Augustana College. This newspaper was Lutheran and read chiefly by Lutherans. The other church groups, Swedish, Methodist, Baptist, and the Mission Covenant, started their own newspapers and church publications.

As more immigrants came to America many newspapers were published independently of the churches. Among these were *Nordstjernan, Svea, Svenska Amerikanaren, Svenska Amerikanska Posten,* and *Vestkusten.* The most popular was *Svenska Amerikanska Posten.* It was published in Minneapolis, Minnesota, and at one time had the largest circulation of any Swedish newspaper in the world. Its editor and owner was Swan J. Turnblad.

The next most popular was *Svenska Amerikanaren.* Today it is the only Swedish language newspaper published in the United States. Its name has been changed to *Svenska Amerikanaren —Tribunen.* It is published every Wednesday by the Swedish American Newspaper Company in Chicago.

There are three English language magazines which publish material of interest to the Swedish people, *The American Swedish Monthly, The American Scandinavian Review,* and *The Vasa Star,* the official monthly journal of the Vasa Order of America. It is published in both the Swedish and English languages.

The early writers were clergymen, journalists, and educators, for these were the educated people among the immigrants. A well-known name among them was Oscar L. Stromberg, a Methodist minister. He was a prolific writer of poems, short stories and novels. Another writer was Ernst Skarstedt, the editor of various newspapers. He wrote both prose and poetry and did more than anyone to make Swedish-American literature known.

Fredrika Bremer, an important Swedish novelist, was the first professional writer in Sweden to come to the United States. This was in 1849. Her novels were translated into English and widely read by many people, including such noted American writers as Longfellow, James Russell Lowell, and Walt Whitman. As she traveled in America she wrote make-believe letters describing what she saw and experienced in this country. When she returned to Sweden she had those letters published in a book. This book helped stimulate immigration to the United States, and to Minnesota in particular.

A present-day Swedish writer whose books and magazine articles have had much influence in the United States is Gunnar Myrdal, a Swedish economist and politician. In 1938 he came to the United States to conduct research on the Negro people for the Carnegie Corporation. As a result of his study he wrote the book *An American Dilemma, The Negro Problem and Modern Democracy*. This volume had much influence on the decisions of the United States Supreme Court relating to the civil rights of Negroes.

Much verse and prose was written by the immigrants. The themes were usually nature, religion, and the longing for their homeland. They also described the hardships they had to endure, the sacrifices they made, and their plans and dreams for the future. In his book *Now the Prairie Blooms*, Albin Widen describes the struggles, hardships and hopes of a group of settlers in Minnesota. America's best known writer of Swedish descent, Carl Sandburg, was both a poet and a historian. His six-volume biography of Abraham Lincoln is widely read; the part called *The War Years* won a Pulitzer prize in 1940. Sandburg was also a speaker, a radio commentator, and a singer and collector of folksongs. Born in Galesburg, Illinois in 1878, Sandburg died in 1967.

Carl Sandburg, poet and historian, celebrating his 75th birthday.

Minnesota has many authors of Swedish descent. One who has written numerous books for teen-age girls is Annette Turngren. *Copper Kettle* and *Shadows into Mist* are two of her pioneer stories which are in most school libraries. Miss Turngren was the associate editor for *Calling All Girls,* a girls' magazine, and now works for the *New York Times.*

7. *Medicine*

During the 16th and 17th centuries in Europe the barber's craft was connected with medicine and surgery. Many ailments were thought to be caused by bad blood. Therefore one common remedy for many diseases was to bleed the patient. Barbers were trained to do this. They were known as barber-surgeons.

The barber pole that we see today outside of barbershops is a symbol of this. The white represents the bandages used to bind up the arm after bleeding. The red stripe represents the blood and the round top of the pole represents the basin to catch the blood.

The first barber-surgeon in the Delaware colony of New Sweden was Jan Petersen. The best known and most prominent was Timon Stidden. The change of climate and hard work caused much sickness among the early colonists. Dr. Stidden was ordered to New Sweden to take care of the sick colonists and soldiers. This was in 1656. The metal case in which he carried his instruments is still in the possession of one of his descendants. For many years the colonists depended upon European trained barber-surgeons and doctors. The young men in America who chose medicine as a profession were trained in Europe.

The first medical diploma given in America was to John Archer in 1768. It was granted to him by Adam Kuhn, a professor of medicine in the College of Philadelphia. Adam Kuhn had studied medicine and botany at the University of Upsala, Sweden under the famous botanist Linneaus.

Prominent Swedish doctors in the 19th century included the two brothers, Alfred and Moreton Stille. Alfred Stille discovered the difference between typhus and typhoid fever. Dr. William Keen of Philadelphia became known as the Dean of American Surgeons. He wrote *System of Surgery*, the eight volumes of which were a standard work. Dr. Johan Ouchterlony came to America in 1857 at the age of 19. He received his medical degree in 1860 and became an army surgeon in the Civil War. After the war he was a lecturer on clinical medicine at the University of Louisville, Kentucky. His skill and outstanding accomplishments gave him national recognition. He helped establish the Louisville Medical School and was the principal instructor of medicine in that institution from 1882 until his death in 1908.

Before the year 1880 there were very few Swedish doctors who came to the immigrant settlements in the Middle West. The immigrants were poor, and transportation and communication were also very poor, so professional men were not eager to go into those communities.

After the land was settled and towns and cities were built, Swedish doctors came to the Middle West. Some had been trained in Europe, others had received training in the eastern cities of the United States. The immigrants were happy to receive them for they wanted doctors who spoke the Swedish language. These doctors not only took care of the sick, they became leaders in the church and in the community where they lived. One of these pioneer doctors was Dr. John Eklund, who came to Duluth in 1885. He developed a large medical and surgical practice. He was one of the founders of St. Luke's Hospital, which serves much of northeastern and northern Minnesota. In addition to his medical practice, he was prominent in civic affairs and did much to build the city of Duluth.

Other doctors who have helped build hospitals were Drs. Carl Reignell, A. E. Anderson, and Alfred Lind. They were leaders in founding the Swedish Hospital in Minneapolis. In St. Paul, Minnesota, Dr. Erik Lundholm and Olof Sohlberg were leaders in building the Bethesda Hospital in that city.

Dr. Carl A. Hedblom, famous for his research work on chest surgery.

Dr. Robert Earl is another pioneer doctor. He began his practice in general surgery in St. Paul after he graduated from the University of Minnesota. The Earl Clinic which he established, and which is owned now by his descendants, is one of the important medical clinics in St. Paul.

Dr. Kristian G. Hansson was born in Sweden but received his medical degrees from Cornell University Medical College. He specialized in physical therapy. He became nationally known for his work in that field and in the field of orthopedic surgery.

After the year 1900 medical schools were established in the Middle West. Those schools and the Mayo Clinic in Rochester, Minnesota, attracted many young students and doctors of Swedish descent. One of these was Dr. Carl A. Hedblom. He was born in Iowa and received his medical degree from Harvard University. After holding several positions as professor of surgery he came to the Mayo Clinic. Here he established a department for chest surgery. He became known internationally for the hundreds of articles he has written on chest surgery and especially chest surgery for tuberculosis.

A noted eye, ear, nose and throat specialist is Dr. Anderson Hilding of Duluth. In addition to his practice, he has been an assistant at the University of Minnesota Medical School and at the Mayo Clinic. He has done extensive research work and written numerous articles on sinus and respiratory ailments.

The Swedish immigrants have not founded any medical schools. They have, however, built many hospitals. Many of these were established by church groups. The Lutherans have built and maintain hospitals in Omaha, Nebraska, Des Moines, Iowa, and St. Paul, Minnesota. They built the Augustana Hospital in Chicago. There is also a Swedish Hospital in Brooklyn, New York, and one in Minneapolis. These, however, are not affiliated with any church.

Physiotherapy and Swedish massage were first introduced in Sweden by physical culture specialists. They were brought to America in the 1880's. At first those treatments were used most frequently by athletes. However, people soon became aware that the treatments were good for arthritis, paralysis of various kinds, nervous disorders, muscular ailments and also for reducing purposes.

8. *Music and Entertainment*

The Swedes have produced many concert singers, opera stars, and vocalists that are nationally and internationally famous. Quartets, male choruses, mixed choruses, and choirs can be found in every Swedish community. A cappella singing was first introduced in America by the Scandinavians.

Most American-Swedish homes have some musical instrument, usually a piano. To the Swedish people a piano or an organ is more than a piece of furniture. It is an instrument to be used and enjoyed.

The history of the early Swedes in America contains the names of good pianists, organists, teachers, and conductors of music. The immigrants brought with them their folk songs and hymns. The singing of hymns in church was encouraged and many of the early churches had organs. Some of the early pioneers built organs for their churches.

One of these early organ builders was Gustaf Hesselius, the founder of the American school of painting. As early as 1742, he was known as the first organ builder. He also made the first spinets in America.

The organ in the church constructed by the Janssonites in Bishop Hill was built by one of the members of the colony. The first organ in the Methodist church in that town was also built by a Swede.

A well-known organist, teacher and composer of music was Gustaf Johnson. He was born in Sweden and came to Minneapolis in 1875. There he established a school which he named the Johnson School of Music, Oratory, and Dramatic Art. He was a pioneer in teaching, composing, and directing music groups in the Upper Midwest.

Another prominent composer and music teacher in Minneapolis was J. Victor Bergquist. He was born in St. Peter, Minnesota, and received most of his education in Berlin and Paris. In addition to being an organist in several of the large churches in Minneapolis and teaching music, he composed music for high school students. His outstanding composition is the oratorio *Golgatha.*

One of the most noted American-Swedish composers is Howard Hanson, who was the director of the Eastman School of Music in Rochester, New York. Mr. Hanson composed numerous well-known symphonies, concertos, symphonic poems, and other musical compositions. He was requested by the Metropolitan Opera Company in New York to write the opera *Merry Mount.* His best known symphony is called *Nordic.*

The most famous Swedish concert singer was the soprano Jenny Lind, "The Swedish Nightingale." She came to the United States upon the invitation of P. T. Barnum, the circus owner. He offered her from $1,000 to $2,000 per concert. The first concert was given in New York City and the proceeds amounted to $10,000. Miss

Karen Branzell, well-known singer with the New York Metropolitan Opera, 1923-1944.

Jussi Bjoerling, popular tenor with the New York Metropolitan Opera until his death in 1960.

Kerstin Thorberg, leading contralto with the Metropolitan Opera, 1936-1950.

Birgit Nilsson, a leading contemporary opera singer.

Lind stayed in the United States two and one-half years and gave over 125 concerts in that time. She did not become an American citizen but she gave thousands of dollars to religious and charitable groups for the assistance of Swedish immigrants.

More than 25 singers of Swedish parentage, both men and women, have appeared as opera stars in America. Just a few will be mentioned. Olive Fremstad was born in Sweden and grew up in Minneapolis. She became one of the greatest singers of the Metropolitan Opera in New York. Jennie Morelli (Morelius) often sang in opera with the great Caruso. Karen Branzell, a contralto, sang with the Metropolitan from 1923 to 1944. Jussi Bjoerling, who died a few years ago, was a popular tenor singer.

Those prominent in opera today include Blanche Thebom,

Greta Garbo, one of the great motion picture actresses of all times. She is pictured with Charles Boyer, an American of French descent.

Gloria Swanson, glamour movie star of the 1920's.

Ingrid Bergman, famous movie star, in the role of Joan of Arc.

Inger Stevens, popular star in movies and television.

Kerstin Thorberg, Astrid Varnay and Birgit Nilsson. Some Swedish singers in the past Italianized their names to gain prominence. That is not done today.

Many Swedish actors and actresses have achieved success in the movies. Who can forget the great Swedish actress, Greta Garbo? Warner Oland is remembered, amusingly, for the many pictures he appeared in as the Chinese detective, Charlie Chan. We can name any number who have been popular in the past and still more who appear in our movies today. Among these can be mentioned Anna Q. Nilsson, Nils Asther, Dorothy Peterson, Signe Hasso, Viveca Lindfors, Gloria Swanson, Anna Sten, Ingrid Bergman, Arlene Dahl, Anita Ekberg, Leonard Clairmont, Inger Stevens, Ann Margaret, May Britt, and Richard Carlson.

Richard Carlson, television and screen actor.

Edgar Bergen and Charlie McCarthy, famous movie, radio, and television performers.

In radio and on television, Edgar Bergen is a favorite with young and old. Karl Swenson is well-known, for he has played the title role in two productions about Abraham Lincoln.

Alice Frost, the daughter of a Lutheran pastor from Minnesota, has played the part of Mrs. North in the program *Mr. and Mrs. North.*

9. *Artists and Sculptors*

The first Swedish artist who became well-known in America was Gustaf Hesselius. He arrived in Philadelphia in 1712. Shortly afterwards he painted the altarpiece *The Last Supper* for St. Barnabas' Church. In addition to religious subjects he did many portraits. John Hesselius, his son, was also a prominent painter. His paintings are found in many museums. He gave the first lessons in painting to the noted artist Charles William Peale.

Lars Gustaf Sellstedt was a self-taught artist who became well-known as a portrait painter. He painted pictures of President Millard Fillmore, President Grover Cleveland, and many other famous people. He was the principal founder of the Buffalo Academy of Fine Arts and its director for many years.

Olaf Krantz of the Bishop Hill colony in Illinois was another self-taught artist. His paintings of farm scenes and portraits of

Portrait of Charles Calvert, son of the founder of Maryland, painted in 1761 by John Hesselius.

Portrait of Olaf Broline (grandfather of the author), painted by the primitive artist Olaf Krantz of Bishop Hill, Illinois.

prominent men in the colony are truly primitive American art. The collection has been exhibited in New York City and in Chicago. It is owned by the Illinois Historical Society and is on display in the old colony church in Bishop Hill.

There have been many landscape painters of note among Swedish artists. Birger Sandzen of Lindsborg, Kansas, became very well-known for his paintings of mountain scenes. These paintings are found in the art galleries of Chicago, Washington, D.C., New York, London, Paris, Stockholm and Gothenborg. Sandzen was a teacher and lecturer as well as an artist. He did much to make the Middle West art-conscious.

John F. Carlson and Henry Matson, both of Woodstock, New York, won many prizes for their landscape paintings. Carlson's *Woods in Winter* was purchased by the Corcoran Gallery in Washington, D.C. Matson's *Wings of the Morning* is owned by the Metropolitan Museum of Art in New York.

Carl Oscar Borg of California was another self-taught artist. He became well-known for his paintings and sketches of the homelife of Indians in the Southwest. When the movie producers in Hollywood needed help in reproducing pictures of the Hopi Indian Villages, it was Carl Borg who was called to give them advice. His canvases are found in art galleries in the United States and in Europe.

Several artists painted marine scenes. This was natural for the seafaring Scandinavians. Lieut. Com. Henry Reuterdahl, a marine painter, is one of the best known. Many of his marine paintings are in the Naval Academy at Annapolis.

Anders Zorn, the great Swedish artist, did not become an American citizen but his influence on art in America was great. He came to the United States five times to paint portraits and to exchange ideas with American painters. While in America he painted portraits of Andrew Carnegie, the Deerings in Chicago, President and Mrs. Grover Cleveland, and many prominent people of that time.

The Swedish people have established several art centers. The first one was at Bethany College in Lindsborg, Kansas. Augustana

College in Rock Island has a well-known art department. Chicago has two art societies, The Swedish-American Art Association and the Swedish Artists of Chicago. Minneapolis has the American-Swedish Institute, where yearly exhibits of art are given. This Institute is in the former home of Swan J. Turnblad, the Swedish newspaper owner. Besides his home, he left his entire fortune to the Institute.

Carl Milles, who was born in Sweden but lived most of his adult life in the United States, is the most famous of Swedish sculptors. His huge Indian statue of Mexican onyx, symbolizing peace, stands in the lobby of the City Hall in St. Paul. The *Fountain* at St. Louis and the New Sweden Tercentenary Monument at Wilmington, Delaware are also examples of his work. There are many pieces of his sculpture in other cities in the United States and in Europe.

Francis P. Hedlund from Massachusetts worked with Gutzon Borglum on the Stone Mountain Memorial near Atlanta, Georgia. He also worked as a sculptor carving the faces on Mt. Rushmore in South Dakota.

Wood carving came naturally to the Swedes. In their homeland wood was plentiful. Many of their household utensils such as spoons, forks, and bowls were made of wood. Therefore, skill in wood carving was common among the immigrants. Charles Haage is no doubt the most noted wood carver. He carved fifty statuettes which he named *Spirits of the Forest.* These pieces of sculpture have been exhibited in many cities. Carl Halstahammar was a noted teacher of wood carving. He also lectured on the subject and is the author of books on the art of wood carving. John Torrell helped carve decorations for the Tribune Tower and the Furniture Mart in Chicago. He also made the designs on the doors of the elevators in the Palmolive Building in Chicago.

The comic strip *Harold Teen* was originated by Carl Ed. He was born in Moline, Illinois, of Swedish parents.

Gustaf Tenggren was a book and film artist. He has illustrated many well-known books. He has also been art director for the Walt Disney Studios in Hollywood.

Indian God of Peace, showing detail of peace pipe.

Indian God of Peace by Carl Milles in the City Hall at St. Paul, Minnesota.

Indian God of Peace, showing detail of the head.

10. *Religion and Religious Leaders*

The religious unrest in Sweden during the early 1800's was not the main cause for the mass emigration at that time. However it was a strong contributing reason, particularly in the northern provinces.

When the Delaware colony was settled the State Church of Sweden took responsibility for the spiritual welfare of the settlers. Ordained, well-educated ministers were sent over to establish congregations and build churches. The first of these was Old Swedes Church at Wilmington. The State Church of Sweden continued to do this work even when the colony was taken over by the English. After 1789, when the colonies became the United States, Old Swedes Church and others in Delaware became American Protestant Episcopal churches.

No further attempt was made to establish Swedish churches in America until the middle of the 19th century, when Swedes began to settle in the Mississippi River Valley. Then new congregations were founded, churches built, and conferences and synods organized.

The largest immigrant church group were Lutherans. When the first settlers arrived there were no Lutheran pastors to help them organize congregations. The State Church of Sweden opposed emigration and paid no attention to the spiritual needs of the emigrants. This indifference of the clergy in Sweden to the church in America was a help rather than a hindrance. It made the settlers independent and self-reliant. As a result, all religious groups from Sweden adopted a general American pattern. They established Sunday schools. They made their churches the center for social and educational activities as well as for worship. In some instances even the Lutheran liturgy was changed.

The pioneer Lutheran pastor in the Middle West was Rev. Lars P. Esbjorn. He accompanied a group of immigrants that arrived in New York in September 1849. They were not dissenters, but had rebelled against certain State Church practices. They wanted to settle together in a community but had no definite place in mind. Rev. Olaf Hedstrom of the *Bethel Ship* in New York persuaded them to go to Andover, Illinois. This they did and it was here that Rev. Esbjorn formed the first Swedish Lutheran congregation in the Middle West, with a membership of about 40 people.

Rev. Esbjorn worked hard to collect money to build a church. He went East and made a personal appeal to the great Swedish singer Jenny Lind, who gave him $1,500. With that sum, and other small sums of money added to it, a church was built in 1851. It is now a museum and was named the Jenny Lind Chapel in 1948.

In 1852 a second Lutheran congregation was organized in Galesburg, Illinois by Rev. Tuve Hasselquist. A few years later he organized the first Lutheran congregation in Chicago.

As more Swedish immigrants came to the Middle West, more and more Lutheran congregations were organized. They grew rapidly and soon there was a need for an organization to bind them together. With the help of Rev. Esbjorn and others, Rev. Hasselquist organized all the Swedish Lutheran congregations into one body called the Augustana Lutheran Synod. Rev. Hasselquist became its first president. As more congregations were founded the Augustana Synod became quite a large organization, exerting much influence on both education and religion among the Swedes in America.

Another pioneer worker in the Lutheran Church was Rev. Eric Norelius. At the age of 17 he came from Sweden to Andover, Illinois. After being ordained a Lutheran minister he went to Vasa, Minnesota, where he organized the first Swedish Lutheran congregation in that state. He also helped organize an academy which later became Gustavus Adolphus College. For many years he was the only Lutheran preacher who ministered to the spiritual needs of the Swedish pioneers in Minnesota. He is a fine example of the many pioneer religious leaders of all faiths who devoted their lives to the people's welfare.

A prominent recent leader was Dr. Reuben Youngdahl, pastor of Mt. Olivet Church in Minneapolis. Dr. Youngdahl, who died in 1968, was an author, lecturer, and civic leader. Dr. Edgar Carlson is

Dr. Reuben K. Youngdahl, prominent clergyman, author, and radio commentator.

president of Gustavus Adolphus College and a leader in education. Rev. Milton Bergstrand is a noted youth leader and lecturer.

In 1962 the Augustana Synod united with the United Lutheran Synod (of German origin) and with two smaller synods to form the Lutheran Church in America. This new church body has 3,200,000 baptized members and 6,200 congregations. It is the largest organization of Lutheran churches in the United States.

In the early 1840's Gustaf Unonius, a very well-educated man and a writer, came from Sweden with his family and a few friends and settled in Wisconsin. He bought a large tract of land, hoping to establish a colony.

As the settlers increased in numbers, Unonius decided he would be their minister, but the Lutheran Church refused to recognize him for he had not been ordained. Thereupon Unonius joined the Protestant Episcopal Church and founded a small congregation of Swedish Episcopalians in his community. He later organized one in Chicago, for he felt there was a great need for a Swedish church where poor, sick, and bewildered immigrants could go for comfort, solace and advice. Unonius also appealed to Jenny Lind for funds.

She graciously donated $1,500 towards building a church, and $1,000 for a silver communion service.

After Unonius returned to Sweden in 1888 a few Swedish Episcopal congregations were organized in Minnesota, Illinois, and in New York State. They were never large and after they had fulfilled their mission as spiritual helpers for the pioneers they united with the American Episcopal Church.

The first Swedish Methodist preacher in America was Rev. Olaf G. Hedstrom. He became converted to the Methodist faith shortly after he came to the United States in 1822. For several years thereafter he was a missionary for the American Methodist Church working among the Swedish settlers in New York and the New England States.

In 1845 the Methodist Church in New York City purchased a ship and placed it in the harbor. This was to serve as a meeting place for the incoming Swedish immigrants and for Swedish sailors. Here they were given Bibles, Testaments, advice, and money if they needed it. Rev. Olaf Hedstrom was put in charge of the work and the ship was given the name *Bethel Ship*.

Most of the immigrants who visited the *Bethel Ship* were eager to settle in the Middle West, where land was plentiful. Accordingly, Rev. Hedstrom advised them to go to Victoria, Illinois where his brother, Jonas, also a Methodist preacher, was living. The first Swedish Methodist church service was held in a log cabin at Victoria, Illinois with five Swedish immigrants attending. In 1852 a permanent congregation was formed and a church was built.

The Methodist congregations grew slowly, even though they had many well-educated leaders who worked among the people as preachers and educators. In 1942 the Swedish division and the English division of the Methodist Church became one church body. There had been, at one time, as many as 250 Swedish Methodist congregations served by over 200 ministers. They also possessed a publishing house and a seminary. All have been united with the English-speaking Methodist Church.

The first Baptist to be banished from Sweden, because he disagreed with the teachings of the State Church, was Fredrick O. Nilsson, a missionary preacher. He was also the last one to be banished, for the law regarding membership in the Lutheran Church was changed due to much international objection. Mr. Nilsson went from Sweden to Germany where he worked as a missionary for a few years. Later he came to America and organized Baptist congregations in Iowa and Minnesota. One of these early congregations was near where the Twin Cities are today.

About the same time that Mr. Nilsson left Sweden, Mr. Gustaf Palmquist, a school teacher, came to America to serve as a pastor in a Lutheran church at Galesburg, Illinois. While in that town he became converted to the Baptist faith and was at once ordained as a preacher. He was sent to work among the Swedes in Rock Island, Illinois and there organized the first Swedish Baptist church in America.

Like the Swedish Methodists, the Baptist congregation grew slowly. By 1949 there were 325 congregations with 42,000 members. Since that date they have united with the English-speaking division of the Baptist Church. However, as a separate group they made worthy contributions by building schools, colleges, churches, and homes for the aged and for orphans. Their publishing house published Sunday school materials, books, devotionals, and a weekly newspaper.

Several smaller groups of dissenters broke away from the Swedish Lutheran Church after they came to America. They chose various names such as Lutheran Mission Church, Mission Society and Mission Synod. Since they had much the same doctrine, they finally decided to unite. In 1885 they joined into one church group and took the name Evangelical Mission Covenant Church. They chose Carl A. Bjork as their president. The new church body prospered. From a beginning of 47 small congregations in Iowa and Illinois it has grown to 524 churches with a membership of 63,154.

One of the best known leaders of this church group was Rev. Erik A. Skogsbergh. He was well-educated, a talented speaker and an able executive. He built schools and churches which he called "tabernacles." The tabernacle he built in Minneapolis, Minnesota, is today one of the large churches in this area. Skogsbergh's dynamic personality and his sincere faith won many converts for his church.

The influence of the church on the Swedish people in America was great both spiritually and culturally. To the immigrants it became a social institution which helped them adjust to a new and difficult environment. Through the church, contacts were made with men and women who spoke the Swedish language and who had a similar background of experience. This helped them to succeed in their new way of life. Through the churches, colleges, Sunday schools, and church publications, the children of the immigrants were taught the language, customs, traditions, and culture of Sweden. One of these customs that has been handed down to us is the Christmas celebration.

To the Swedish people, the Christmas holidays were the most festive, joyous, and sacred of the whole year. The American Christmas is richer and more sacred for the elaborate decorations in homes, shops, and streets and the Christmas carols that come to us through the customs of the Swedish people.

However, it is the churches, colleges, seminaries, hospitals, and homes for the aged that are the lasting monuments to the faithful and dedicated pioneer laymen and preachers.

Conclusion

Between 1860 and 1920 over one million Swedes came to America. They settled in every section of our country, except the southeastern states bordering on the Gulf of Mexico and the Atlantic Ocean. The 1960 census lists the total of first and second generation Swedes living in the United States as 1,046,942. Millions more trace their American ancestry back beyond two generations.

Swedish immigration to America has now almost ceased. For several years the quota has not been filled. This is due to the progress which Sweden has made since 1840 when mass emigration from that country began.

Today Sweden is a highly industrialized country with sufficient employment for everyone willing to work. The people enjoy a high standard of living. Both men and women have the right to vote and the government is as democratic as any modern government can be.

The contributions which the Swedes have made to our American way of life are many in the various trades, occupations, and professions which they entered. They have not excelled in all fields of endeavor. However, since the first Swedes came to America in 1638, they have made worthy contributions in engineering, invention, and the applied sciences. Due to their restless, inquiring spirits they have been in the forefront among the makers of that which is modern in life today.

As soon as the Swedish immigrants found a place to live they were eager to become citizens of the United States, and therefore they were quickly and thoroughly Americanized. They have shown a deep sense of responsibility and civic pride in local, state, and national government. They have made fine Americans.

ABOUT THE AUTHOR...

PERCIE V. HILLBRAND is descended from the Swedish pioneers whose story she tells in this book. Miss Hillbrand received her Bachelor of Science and Master of Arts degrees from the University of Minnesota. She has been a teacher, principal, and a supervisor of teacher training. Her position before retirement was State Supervisor of elementary schools for the Minnesota Department of Education. At present, she devotes herself to writing and traveling. She is also the co-author of *Our Minnesota*, a history of the state.